David Greenslade has many books of poetry, prose
and non-fiction in print. He works for the Open
College Network and has received scholarships from
the British Council and the Arts Council of Wales.
He writes in Welsh and in English and his poems have
been translated into several languages.

PARTHIAN

# WEAK EROS

## David Greenslade

PARTHIAN

Parthian
The Old Surgery
Napier Street
Cardigan
SA43 1ED
www.parthianbooks.co.uk

ISBN 1-902638-26-3

Typeset in New Sabon by NW

Printed and bound by Dinefwr Press, Llandybie

With Support from the Parthian Collective

The publishers would like to thank the Arts Council of Wales
for support in the publication of this volume

A cataloguing record for this book is available from the British
Library.

| Cover Design: | Marc Jennings |
| Art: | Keith Bayliss |

# *RHIANNON*

Poetry

Burning Down the Dosbarth (Y Lolfa)
Old Emulsion Customs (Y Wasg Israddol)
March (in Welsh, Y Wasg Israddol)
Yr Wyddor (in Welsh, Gwasg Gomer)
Creosote (Two Rivers Press)
Each Broken Object (Two Rivers Press)
Cambrian Country (Gwasg Carreg Gwalch)

Fiction

Celtic Hot Tub (Gwasg Carreg Gwalch)

**Thanks** to the editors of the following magazines:
The Pharos (USA), Planet, Poetry Wales, Rowndy House, Runes (USA), The Unruly Sun, Vines (USA), Waterlog, Wolf's Tale.
*A Love Letter* was previously published as a pamphlet from Y Wasg Israddol. *The Sorcerer Receives a Cutte* previously appeared as a pamphlet from Two Rivers Press.

# Contents

7

## Our Perfumed Book

We endured
each adulterous whisper,
cut perfumed paper,
folded wild
unbalanced letters.
I tore your envelopes,
steering their edges
deep into my hands,
each word
looking forward
to when my letter
opened, never
to be read
by me again.
Years later your son
gave my letters back,
handing them over
in a cardboard box.
I remember every time
we reached across – how
our nervous songsheet grew –
rewriting dreams,
phonecalls, nights
away, long drives,
waiting in the pub –
what we could
and could not change.
The chances we took
haunting each page
of our unpublished book.

## Paper

We stood
on the chalk
of a steep vineyard,

what we wanted
awkwardly
welcoming –

each word, an egg
between our teeth,

a summer hailstorm
over a slowly changing sea.

Wading through dunes
of broken oystershells,
until we wrote again.

## That Night


Your husband would be gone
                    we
    wanted
to try each other out.
You said it
                    quickly
            but
        it wasn't just your idea,
            I'd also been lifting
        you up to the light,
flirting
    with
        drops of wine
            on your skin.
            We bought a thousand drinks,
                            some for your knees,
                            more for your breasts.
            You set a dare
            below my navel,
                            where my thighs
            became only a little
confident;
                not quite as full of myself
            now that our mutual swagger
            cowered
            in a corner of the sofa.
                    You flattened
        into a cold murmer
                            admitting
            we were happiest in beds
            where we belonged.
            My souvenir –
            a red bow
            from the keystone of your bra.

## The Car Behind

I see her
    driving the car
        behind,
            seeing
forces me
    to look
            again
        at the speed she opens up
            veiled
        in my unreflected look,
wanting to
leap
            at all the offers
    of another woman,
        racing
        where I always
            might have been.

## Confetti

In case you'd forgotten
how much of an idiot
I could be for you,
in front of eighty people
any one of whom
would commit as much
if this same sudden madness hit them,
I waved at you like a child
waving at a train.

You inclined your head
and whispered my name.

Another time, equally amazed,
we met by accident in town.
Clowning puppeteers
fixed my eyes on yours,
forcing you to stand exactly in my way.

The sensible words we used!
Sand drying out a bowling green,
just enough to bring our game along.
Silence crashed
whatever else we meant
to do that day into burning flakes.

Confetti.

I had to try again
and broke a meeting to see you,
guarding my tongue
until your smile forced
all kinds of sayings out of me.

Clearly I was living
in the grounds of a park
whose paths
could be quickly closed.

At least I'd opened a gate
for the kiss
I still may never get from you.

I returned to work,
my long want moving forward
to drink from the straw
of having known you.

## Her Eyes

She doesn't sell a lot –
jackdaws raid the fruit boxes
stealing grapes
while she sits inside
selling cigarettes
to schoolkids. Mumbling.
They think she's mad.
Small veins on her cheeks
finer than the down
on primrose stems,
white hair trailing – held back
from her face by the clips
of walkman headphones.
She didn't always sing
or limp. She gave up circle
dancing and took up singing
when she couldn't go outside
as much. The shop folds in on her.
She has the brightest, bluest eyes.

## Gloves

Last night,
how much damage?

No bruises,
no marriage overturned.

You were annoyed
when I admired

the way
you put on gloves

showing no restraint
and still can't;

my eyes – crazy
like a moth – dancing

against the leather
of your fluttering hands.

## Second Date

I'd had a good day
two hours in the gym, sauna,
swim, then a massage.

Cooked.

A walk to the bookshops
and a good find:
*Hopkinsons Boilers and Gauges*;
coloured prints
photographs of British industry, 1959;
Britannia Works, Huddersfield.
Foundrymen wearing waistcoats and ties.
The workshop of the world.

Then a nap.
An honest nap
with a bottle of sparkling water,
*New Scientist*
fallen across my chest –
an article on pneumatics and hydraulics.

That night, dinner –
wearing a blazer and white shirt
open at the neck;
my heaviest gold chain,
gold watch, gold ring
shining in the mirror.

She wore red and white.
When I had the chance
I checked her handbag.

I felt serene
surrounded by plenty of knives and forks,
the waiters' *guéridon* gleaming nearby.
When she put both her hands
on my arm and asked
how I spent my time –
knowing that, as she did,
I spent most days working out –

I felt a wet, little valve pop
somewhere near my ankle
(where there used to be a wing)
and all my warm, tumescent air
start hissing.

She didn't notice
until my waxy, flattening hand,
growing tired – like
a cold, sandy airbed
deflating on the beach –
failed to lift a fork.

My thighs let me down twenty five millimetres
over fifteen minutes.
I started to slide
under the restaurant table.

She wouldn't have it.

Calmly chewing a crust of bread,
sipping the wine,
scarlet nails
near a red, impassive mouth,
she reached, tapped me on the head
and grabbed my hair.

I see what you're doing
and you can stop it;
take a walk,
smell the flowers,
tell me about your car,
crayon on the tablecloth;

do whatever you have to
no matter what,
even if it means getting the chef
to grill the bottoms of your feet –
even if it means a picnic of utter filth –
just do it.

Don't go sinking among these table legs,
serviettes, lost coins, breadcrumbs.
What kind of date is that?

## It was Good to See You

You came into my festival stall.
I was selling
            flowers and books,
your dress unbuttoned
                        from high on the waist
    almost to the hem.
Don't tell me you didn't know.
            Books, flowers,
        paintings
    and the crowd
made you happy;
        breathless
about the respectable
        committee meeting
    where you'd been,
    the round pearl
    of your abdomen
            hatching from your dress,
    its satin burst
            forced everything
aside.        All the field
    had seen it.
                I loved imagining
    you sail the muddy
    duckboards – button
        by button
            unfastening
                        as you
    made for our tent.
It was good to see you.

20

## Cake

Your body
resembled
a folded cake
the kind I rarely buy
soft    overlooked;
with a glazed
finish in the cake shop
window
where
I saw it
one Saturday afternoon,
almost hardening,     steady,
worth breaking
my reflection in the door
to go inside
and get it –
my fingers hungrier
than I realised
slobbering
tearing,
just as you
know what you want
licking your fingers
and lips
to get it.
The relaxed
athletic reaches
our bodies
displayed
knowing how

much the other
would regret
not getting everything
there was;
how eagerly
the neglected
always
offer up a little more.

## Five Children

He was built like an axe,
skin the colour of beech,
curved, lean,
hair shaved both sides of his head,
a cropped mat on top, evenly
growing out,
made his profile fierce.

His body swarmed like bees over mine,
my arms rippled over his.
Sand dunes were our favourite,
horse grass around us,
on a footpath
careless, too impatient
to go any further,
voices nearby.

My father made me tell who it was.
He reached down to slap
my legs, pinching my arms,
when he slapped my cheek I knew it was over.
You'll get this, then you'll see
pressing his fist to my belly.
My mother pulled my hair – screaming, "Who?"
They weren't surprised,
so I said it only once.

I remember every time
– beautiful daylight –
now I stand at the back gate
aged fifteen, hair
cut straight across my forehead
five months pregnant, waiting.

You live two streets away

but I never see you.
Next door, budgies whine like engines,
dogs run down the street,
my body itches in one pink blotch.

His father beat him too,
kneeling on his back, pouring a bottle
of kitchen bleach through the henna in his hair,
gripping the earring in his nose.
His sister told me how he pleaded.

My mother was terrified
when his father walked by one morning
after signing at the curfew desk.
He kicked the bottom panel of our door
and crawled inside. Taking his time. We barricaded
the bedroom. Forget it, he said,
rocking the bannister until it broke.

The baby would keep my name.

When my baby was six months old
mam and dad were working,
my brother came home
with a friend I'd never seen before.
They made me switch the telly off
so they could watch some videos.
My brother came back with towels
and sent me out.
They were getting pissed.
In the film, men bent over a woman
panting so hard I stood near the door
and couldn't look away.

A towel over my brother's lap,
dark bronze bodies on telly,
photographs of me with the baby.
I couldn't leave. My brother
pulled his trousers up
but the other boy kept drinking.
It lasted ages
so I went upstairs.

They brought a bottle of codeine
which I drank, with cider, almost all at once.
When the walls were as soft as elastic bands
his friend did to me
what they'd just seen.
My screams come out in long gooey strings
until my brother ran out to be sick.
I got burned on my back. When they finished
I took my baby down the shops for a walk.
I never saw that boy again. I hope he's dead.

The street looked weird that night.
Every house a trap. Guns, cars, adverts, banks,
complaints, explosions and threats were the stories
I heard from my neighbours' open windows.
Music, drums hissing out of passing cars.
I didn't buy anything. I didn't know
where else to go. My back hurt.
I couldn't talk – bombed,
 stinking from that cough medicine.


A month before my second was born
my brother swallowed his savings – two hundred pills.
Dad found him next morning on the garden path
under the back kitchen window.
We thought he was drunk.
They wanted me to name the baby after him
but I looked for my own flat
and got tested for it.
I called my baby Leonardo
he'd grow up either rich or useless.


Every night I sat at the window
putting drops of lager on the sill
watching for moths.
Pregnant, I started rolling my own.
The baby came out fine. With two kids
mam helped me out and I got a job
but the nights, with no one there,
feeding and changing, gave me mad ideas.

I thought it would be easier to gas us all.
A flat full of nutters. I started adding up.
Cost of the flat, food,
single with kids. I worked it out.
It doesn't take a genius. One of the cleaners
at work kept hiding my clothes,
one day I had to go home in overalls.
He drove behind the bus,
and said he'd leave his wife for me.
When he did
I told him to buy me a packet of fags.

Eighteen, three children
figure like a model on the telly
when I got my jeans on;
every night a couple of cans,
sharp words for any man my father's age.
All sorts calling around. No chance.

The fourth baby was pure pleasure.
Everyone on holidays,
canaries in tune,
even dogs sounded good.
We had all night,
me and a boy I met in town.
Using ice and a needle
he put a tattoo on my hip;
graphics he called it;
a sexy crocodile waving her bikini.

I'd read a book
and told him not to be a stranger,
he could be seeing more of me

after college, in the afternoon;
he had a choice and picked mine.

We bought a parrot.
We gave the children cream and cakes.
One day we walked out
as far as the river
and lay down in the shallow water.

The fifth child was definitely his,
increasing our money.

When I turned forty
I got a job.
A supervisor there
called me iron-face.
I didn't answer,
just thought, she
doesn't know what
she's working for.
Skinny as a railing,
one breast removed,
three grandchildren,
the ten year old
had an epileptic fit
and died.

## We Lived Together

We moved stones
to the edges of our field,

sleeping outdoors in summer.

The sky dense with stars,
the horizon dark

with other voices singing.

We lived together a long time,
sometimes weeping as we ate,

silent as we dug the garden.

I have known finding
and losing her,

both were terrible.

We shared black sand,
many fallen roses,

losing our portion of sleep.

## Keep Fit

Keep drinking
        filtered water,
        visit the gym,
        swim,
smoothe your legs with
                cream,
        one day
        I'll hold you
        and make your body sing
like the strings of a red violin.
        I'll tear
        the stitching from
        your silk armour,
throw
        your shoes
across a hotel room,
        your dainty
watch
        air its swollen tongue
in a shocking cultural pose.
The bed,
        a restless
        couch;
        waking dreams strain
        your fresh
        dismantled sighs
        through every
        vocal exercise –
calling for rest
*and* more,
an excess of pillows,
        salt
        and wine.

## A Letter

What I'll risk for you,
rises. Steps. Mirrors.

Where?
I'm reminded where I stand.

Where?

Your foam smears
the gleam of a hard apple.

I run my tongue on the green skin,
push my skin
over the slow cluttered diary I own.

When will I read a letter
from you again?

This is a seal
between my lips
a paper blade  −

I bleed, froth,
want,
knowing that my hold

on you, cutting me,
turns deeper in you
as I need

you tell me how you
sparkle with the drops
I bring for you.

I risk all shelves
all speeds, all nights
at home for you.

You've told me how
you've folded down
yourself between pages

of the letter,
letting your riot out,
hands knotting

until a thirsty stitch
unhooks
your pen and mine,

an uncensored drink
pouring
the delivered pretext

from room
to secret room.

I want to see you
in a black window,
be with you
in a garden
thick with vines,

condemned
to go for you,
in the same arena,
dead to all of it
except our wet dust;

aching for rest,
rubbing bruised
and purple dreams,
pressing our pain
back to its greedy edge.

Clothes hold, fold
and rewrap you, but
I will wait – where?
forever?

You know.

You're not in time
and I want you.

You're the other side
and I want you

you scare me with God
and I want you.

you infest me with hotels
and I want you

you defeat me with lace
and I want you

you prize my mouth
and I want you

you stretch my house
you scar my limits

breath thought salt
secure you

I have always
wanted you.

## Moving Books

All I had to do was carry books
         to their new shelves,
a converted loft upstairs –
at last
a library
of my own!        When
I came across your letters –
and      a job
         that should have taken hours
became a covenant of holidays.

Each page as brittle as cake,
anniversaries eaten by my eyes;
the books I bought,
even mistakes,
I love them all.

With each thick grab I disappear
             into
Trakl's wolf-green forest,
Nazim Hikmet's red horizon;
Bobi's cow
     rotting in ice-water
like a crazy highball lifted in a dull hotel;
my body drinks and spins from view.

Each handful puncturing
the day
         I bought them,
     where
             and why
I still adore them now.

These little stacks –
       your found letters
            among them –
re-opening
each subtle treasure box,
each glowing scar;
       perfect
       wounds,
            (unpublished)
fermenting through
       the pagination of my hands.

## Lovespoon

Leaving
to walk home,
closing your door
sounded like a train
slowing on the tracks;
my breath
pausing in your hand.
5 am   –   at the bleak
village junction
between shop
and rugby club  –  hips, elbows
quivering from having held
you  so long       lifting
and turning        you
like fresh-made paper.
Your hands  –  spoons
gleaming with oil,
both of us
working       your  clothes  aside.
Where you eased
your open arms,
pressed your face,
rested your knees,
pushed      your feet
against me              we broke
the arm of the couch!   then
me       spinning home
like a weathercock
– touching the leaves –
along
a short cut
between rows of
flowering allotment beans.

## In That Country

In that country
currency was minted
in the shape of keys.

Shoes were
a flimsy bank.

I could take a coin,
turn it
in the ankle
of a beautiful woman,

opening her foot
like an orange
when it meets the frost.

I was a master thief.
I was always poor there.

## By Bike

Taxis, courier
vans give way.
Stolen flowers. The dog
running at his side.
He steps from one
broken pedal –
and waits,
chaining his dog
to a steel & concrete stand;
her bike
hidden
beneath her shirt,
among reeds
at the edge of the world,
folded
in the scallop of her back.

## Lady Writer

She plowed some iron through my blood
and I had to hear her read.
I drove fifty miles one way –
roads cut like bacon rind

above valleys whose names I'd forgotten,
towns and ditches stewing in the rain.
Roundabouts like black squid
spat at my eyes.

Each swish of the wipers,
press of the breaks,
hiss of the airvents nudging me
harder towards her books.

But I was two days late. Her face
on the poster folded in my pocket
had come and gone. Stunned.
Even my saliva tasted wrong.

One minute in the lobby,
one question and I was reminded
what day it was. Friday night for me
instead of Wednesday night for her.

I could have gone dancing,
instead I drove straight home;
a clotted boomerang dripping
down from Blackwood to Cardiff;

rueing my clumsiness with days
always confusing dates and times,
witless, even with a diary,
saying left – waving right.

I played a favourite tape –
arc upon arc of Qawwali music
curving with the unfamiliar road;
lights like orange rivets on the hills,

darkness flattening the bends;
reciting her lines as I raced ahead,
still crazy about what dragged me out
even if I missed it. Even if I missed it all.

## Sharing a Bath

I thought
I was winning
the argument
at least
warming a little
of the frozen ground
but, when it came to a kiss,
you shifted like a glacier.
Even when I knew
what dogma
I was trying to seduce
I couldn't stop.
Let's share a bath?
A practical approach,
a solution
that might undo
your desire
to be
ice.
My tongue
strained to soften
your hard replies,
find some way
of loosening
your mouth
into an avalanche
of hasty bites, thaw
your breasts, turn
your thighs
on a bed
of restless flint.

## Melancholy Ship

When a little passion
  ends   forcing
 a cruel bruise
      onto everything I hold
once fruit
      now
filled with sneers
      and hate.   Missing
your lips on one cheek
    hand on the other;
      gardening the world
with joy;
strapped in what
  might still be hidden
      but you
      found a way of unwrapping it.
  The hangover of this frenzied city
decorating hours wrecked with flags.
      Asleep –
  sweating in one grey lump,
imagining flowers
     near a door   you
     won't open anymore.
Arms twitching across my ribs,
          far
    from
      music
  fire   and   wine.

## Infatuated

                        because
                  I lost my gaze
              in you,
I walk     where your husband
                  couldn't go;
I've never touched you.
      Jealous
            I decide what's best
            for me to see.     I've learned
don't stare the same way twice.
                        Sharp
            when I was seventeen, this coy skill
is bitter now     –     a privatised delight.
Some risk a little of their plenty
                        for one quick smile
                  in another direction.     But
                        every time you think
                        I'm watching
I look somewhere else.

## Dionysian Building Project

The project wasn't working.
     & the director said,
I'm calling in a consultancy.

All hell broke loose.
Bury me in the garden.

I just want to have my back tickled.
Do we have to be perverse?

Who are you calling a pervert,
slackarse.

Listen I'll say what I like,
I know there's a bonus at the end of this,
get smart, double your money.

I still want to go with the boy I loved in school.
Not everyone refused to take their shirts off.

It got messier;
statues of the virgin,
teeth files,
mine looked good in points.
I sent out for a litter of puppies.

What are you doing with those?
After a little blood,
tambourines,
we shared a sombre shower.

Raised more money,
paid the architect; builders
cut our trenches in the ground.

## Leaves

Stretched between
driving to work
and phonecalls
he makes;

threads
of alcohol
credit cards
rooms near the motorway

spin from his stomach
weak on a diet
of whisky and chips.

At home,
a forgotten hedge,

the dining room table
withers;

neither one of them
ever stirs its leaves.

## It Slipped Away

It slipped away from us
bolting into something
we couldn't eat
or recognise,
              a country
where it wasn't safe
to sleep
              or wake up
anymore;

drinking from
a blue and white saucer
that once went under
a blue and white tea cup
broken in a rage –

even candles
struggle there.

Grooming its hair,
stitching its seams,
grinding its teeth
on clams and sugar cane,

this lousy compound
where we live
denies the plants
their water.
              Neglected –
what happened
to our blanket
under the stars,
              our bed
at the top of the stairs?

## The Hundred Homes

How can she
know
what you're
thinking
when you don't
talk to her?
Why should she
press
your tired shoulders
with her thumbs?
How can she
dream
what you're
dreaming
if you won't
share her pillow?
If you won't
sip
from the glass she
fills at night?
She already
knows
you've
wandered off.
Her neglected mirror
reflects
a different world from yours.
Every day your best efforts
snap
the hundred homes she almost
made.

**Your Table**

I could have woken
    only
        from hands like yours,
full of daylight and deceit –

finding more
        whatever I had to say.

    Claiming rest,
        laughing like a happy king,
blessing your lips
and their soft
challenge,

        one afternoon
        returning kisses
        to your body
like books to a favourite shelf,
I never looked away again.

You reached your hand
and cooked directly from the field;
        preferring never
    to be kissed, if
        baffled silence
were all that sat around,
        terrified
        by the silver promise of your table.

## Far Away

Far away
you frame her like a view,
imagining the seasons,
hips just so
even though you've never seen.

Getting close
means enduring a fever
of strange leaves drying in the shade
of all the carnivals you dreamed about.

This one finishes with your death.

You don't know if you'll get another life or not.
Risk it – fascination means nothing.
The firm slap of an eyelash isn't much to ask.
If you're lucky she'll put a rice cake in your mouth.

Then you'll feel it, turning inside out,
her love for you, luminous and on display –
changing from far to near.
                              Suddenly as capable
as everything your wildest hopes imagined

you work all night and build a house for her.

Near your house, the same leaves drying,
bright roses straining at the wall. How long
can you keep this garden growing?
and frame the view that fuelled your desire?

## Silk Knots

We were
sweepers
caught between
the pacing carpet
master's calls.
Or were we
just a pair
of skiving janitors
on break?
Our sleeping
bag
thirty eight
silk knots
per inch,
unpicked
to thirty seven.
By morning
we were
weavers
waking from
a torn cocoon.

## Curious Questions

"Tell me,"
said the eminent visiting poet,
"can you dream in Welsh?"
I answered, "No.
Our dreams are silent
and, for many, the pictures
are still in black and white;
some can't manage any." "Tell
me," (voice lacquered with red wine)
"do you make love in Welsh?"
I chewed faster on my hazel, flavoured, carmine nuts,
looking for a place to spit,
and again had to answer, "No,
making love in Welsh
is impossible. At a certain stage
quite early in the approach
we resort to finger signals
which becomes a kind of stupor
of gapes and clawing. If
it happens – afterwards, the female
hits the male across the side of his head
with a wooden big tent peg, which mothers
pass to their daughters adolescent when
they reach their teenage muddled years.
When it's over, blood returns
to the tongue and jaw and we talk, again –
usually about renewal urban, policies transport
and the measures traditional
of our ancient poetry clicking.
But yes, of course you're right, we neither
have manifest nor latent dream content,
nor foreplay, nor intercourse sexual in Welsh."

## Your Closet

How could I love you
                without hands and feet?
        Impossible.
        Reaching for ghosts
                when everything
                        I love of yours
                falls
                        into fingerprints.
        When you were out
        I looked
                through your closet,
        taking down
                your clothes;
        sleeves,
hems, ending in air.
        Your body calls these phantoms back
        and I imagine every pore,
                each hidden fold.
        Your empty dresses
                shock and assault
        me
                show
                how clearly I couldn't put them on
        but want to.
                        Better than wearing
        when they half cover you
                underlining, concealing,
        then I move between
                who you are
                        and who I dream about.
        Bright objects whirl about me,
                        gems
                                around a crown
                that never has enough.

# Voice

I found you – one soprano
          out of many –
     at a conference of hymns
and left you near the lifts
          at the bottom of a firm
goodbye;
     but you returned
   making phonecalls
breaking the nets of a contented island.
          I loved the foam you spilled
     and played with the idea of seeing you
   only having met you once.
          I still hear your invitation
where I used to keep my head.
     *Tease-comet. Murmur.* I make pet names
     for you because a million names
   are easier than agreeing to meet you.
Nothing feels safe, when
          pressing my hands
against your breasts could be night
          following a haunted day.
     Sweeter than sleep
          I heard you singing in a forest
suddenly as red as fingernails.
   You showed how easily
     the brittle get raided;
          your complex song
               stretching its throat towards me.

## Foot Massage

Your feet
strapped in tan
almost golden
yellow sandals,
rest
in the easy sofa
of my arms;
as I stroke
one
I trace
the other
with my eyes.
Knowing
I'm greedy
you take
both sandals off.
I rob
their pale
economy.
Spent,
we both
lie busted
on the floor.

# The Sorcerer Receives a Cutte

To Virginia, where
our host at harboure Capt Foyte
eavesdropping shamelessly at our intereste in Plantes
recommendes we walk three nights
to a Tusscarraura tracte inland

where will we witness how Forestes are cleared
by Fowle and Swine
also how plots around
what fewe indigineouse herbal Plantes
maye spreade and flourishe
aided where horse and cow do dung,
likewise the slurye of human waste.

Much impressed
although Moffat disgusted
at the brazeness of the settlement's female servantes;
I instruct that he 'put Himselfe in their Condition'
at which he guffaws as tho it was a joak.

I am approved and singe and jigge
and grinde goode simples that may tumefy a man
when he cannot so much as haill from shippe.

I guess correctly that knowledge of these
Tobbaccow, nutteye beenes and succatow
was taughte and so request that we
maye meete a savage Doctor and all agree.

The Doctor faire in Hispanish yet clumsy
in our Englishe
(which again doth anger inordinately my friende

whom I resolve to kylle
if he continue
since he discomforteth me more tiresome
thus than sleeping as we do togethere)

proclaimes to us – that which we cleape Doctor
he would name a Prince
and other words so manifold and odd
that in the ende I interfere and state were he in England
he would be condemned as a magiciane
and so we all laugh heartily and he agrees
that should his Magicke faile he would be burned
so burning is a fate I tell him awaites me at home.

I am offered a tattw, small cuttes
which do cover the savage Prince's body as completely
as a mappe of Plymouth couvereth
the tabel of foule Webster the Sheriffe's Constable
as he plots his villanye on me at home;

this time I laughe but my native Doctor scowles.
Foyte, Moffat and I goe outside
since I am dizzily intrigued.

Sure, it would restore my Powers,
resist sayes Foyte but Moffat
sensing that thus he maye be ridde of me
dares me ahead "you will gaine" he sayes
and I agree "but where" I aske
already I am in danger to be burned?

Why, on your Arse, sayes Moffatte
and angrilye I tell him thus –
my arse goode friend may be far concealed from thee
but often I sit on it
and his wounds would pester me
for all they provided
jollity to thee.

We tooke a drinke and returned to the fire of the cabinne.
I undressed,
he felt me as a physicke would
and seeing I was plump about the shoulder and the hip
did shew me the appalling bestiary
that ran about his limbes.

I dribled in delight and ordred
my oggling companions out,
mouths agape like taryee caskes,
their dismay inflamed me more,
so on each thigh he spat
and rubbed my legge with paste.
I thoughte the paine would be my shame –
each scallopped wound of his inflamed, old and swollen
must have hurte – as childishly
I waited for the careful stabbes;
but then he gave a cutlet of strange meate
for me to chewe
grained with herbes and brittle twigges,
elabrately he instructed me to masticate
and to vomit back the paste into my mouth
and masticate again
until suddenly I adorred the vulgar cabin
and adorred the flames and longed for the Maide
who waited on us to walk through the door.

When he noticed how my rod thus twitched
the savage take his knife and did gouge my legge,
I would have laughed had he not thrust
an entire coal in it and gouged but daintily again;

this was no Sport,
at his devotion I was crewdely touched,
ungainly and inept
tears crept into my mouth
and no longer to the Maid
my whimsy leapt
but to Venus and my stoney birthplace
where my Mother damme who by Hallucination
I saw disown me as the very Deville.

Thus I had fainted.

My owne bloode woke me droppinge
from the finger of my careful friend
and my astonished Europeans
who saw my legges swollen and deformed,

a Moon on one thighe
the Sun on another,
as I had requested.

Perhaps for our delight,
mollification or dismay,
the Indian took a finest sailing needle
and when he pushed it clear through his flesshy Eare
he set my gifte, a Rodde of Silver, in it
staring at me boldly as he did.

So drugged that the spinning
Baillye could not stand still
I admired him and bade my friends unclasp my handes.

When he had gone
I tooke three tottes of Brandy
when two would serve,

Prudence I could manage
but as my Woundes confinced
restrainte was ever a Difficultye for me.

## Slightly Uptight

I know we are all naked under our clothes
but some are more naked than others.
I mean did you see that blue dress last week,
hanging to the ankles I know,
but sleeveless and tight.
I saw her near the Temple door, lift both arms
stop, turn, emphasising thighs, hips, abdomen,
then break two small leaves
from a branch above her head.
When I go to the beach I don't take off my shirt
until I actually run to the water.
I can just imagine the sand
clinging where she sits,
lotion in a basket at her side,
children nesting in her lap like animals.
Once, we were alone together in my car,
she'd bought a locket for her oldest
daughter and wanted to see it on.
She used the vizor mirror,
taking her own necklace off,
asking me to hold it. I was driving the car
for God's sake, while she sat waving this golden
loveheart before the hollow of her throat.
I dropped her chain with a bony clunk
into the driving console. She tried to get it out,
really fiddling for it among cassettes
and wrappers. She hasn't spoken to me since.
I think she knows she has a bad effect on me.

## Make Salt

Where you sleep
steers its dark wake to me.
I've watched you groom
sheer lust,
                    fencing hours
with your fingertips.
we've danced
            each      un-
                        strapped
            shoulder,
    forced
        our sleeping hips
                    awake;
brewed pungent words,
        helped your white hair
        unspill;
your want-determined tongue
        climb towards
    my own astonished mouth,
        no breeze stirring,
until the night tastes hot
    and we lick
            a gleam of moonlight
from the drying racks.
    "Dart!" you say.
    "Make salt!"
            When morning
cools our cloudy sheets
        a fine sting
        scalds you.

## Coitus at Konarak

I showed you
the bottoms
of my feet,
smooth and pale.
Then I took
a knife and
cut your hair,
arms aching
as though
I were carrying
a blade
of tired dreams
to even further places.
Determined,
my throat
a soak
of heavy sand,
more than once
you winced,
hardening
your eyes
against me,
forcing me
to look
directly at you;
save my breath
for more pink sweat –
the shine of departure
tightening around you.

## Blouse

I want to reach
inside
your white
summer blouse,
steal something
safe
from the lace
of that warm tent.
Your clothes
distract me
from my work –
leather sandals,
straps across your shoulder,
buttons at your wrist.
Your neck lowers
a cotton ladder
to the
thief
waiting at
the open window
of your breasts.

## Complaint

You carried me to your threshold –
        rugs, cushions, tea cups –
    the nets –
            but I couldn't be brought over,
    not even air
            persuaded me.
    Your small lace fence,
        a boundary of kisses
            without limit;
    my hands under your clothes,
                pushing forward
    from daylight to the moon.
            Only when each silk thread
                was tried and broken,
        admitting
        how this desire
        would destroy us,
            could I see and hear
        the domestic range
of your complaints.

## Bird's Nest

Old tales
make a nest
in your face,
your recitations
a curious soup,
young tellings flown.

Bright feathers,
spicy dressing,
new imported broth.

I like what you say –
no telephone
no car
no tv –
better informed
than the best wired news.

Penniless,
teeth leaving
more than one by one,
in the sun
you are brown
to the hinge of your thigh.

Let me taste where
your experience flocks.

Offer me a straw
from the knot
your legs untie.

## White Hair

The white in your hair
    chalks
a new family tree,
a fine nib
    revises
    daylight's lace
    remaining;
    dense looms
      unwritten baskets
      frame
    your eyes.
      Silver stems –
      I love
the script
    fragmented there.

## Fatigue (Chronic)

Although you sleep all day
sick from sleep
sick without it
and we sleep apart at night
I sleep less –
close to the vacuum of losing you.
Illness keeps us both
wandering the obscure paths
of your life story.   Limb
by limb, the heart
of your world is cleared;
numb –  you chew
the hand that reared you.
Vomiting *and* cheering
we count each cold mouthful.
Laughing when I met you
now time itself is agony –
and agony rebuilds you.
When I couldn't face
sleeping on the floor
about to spend another night
knowing how little one
person can cross towards another,
I felt our wedding night
massage the groaning darkness.
I fell asleep screening
your breath
for every trace of change.
Sleep makes no difference.
Eventually you dreamed

of empty plates
spinning on poles,
confused by the tricks
of an unfamiliar hunger.
Soon afterwards
we threw
everything we thought
should be in a pantry
out.
After sleeping for another year,
one day, when you were swallowing
banana mashed with slippery elm,
I noticed how, like sunlight
on a broken windowbox,
your cheeks hinted
they might glow again.

## Tulip Medicine

A ferociouse displaye of teares
when I fail to muster
with either of my maides.

I have not plowed the field
for months, and all entreaties
merely froze a snowbal in my gutte.

Madamme took a poultice
of my expensivest tulippe,
mashinge and rollinge at my table.

She bandaged up my seargeant in it
quite merrily attendinge,
soothinge my groanes and shame.

Uglye she is but goode and folded
her ointmente many times
keeping it warme and changinge it.

"It is a dear medicine" I tolde her.
"Costlier thy ailment" she replied
and shewed her baggye dugges at me.

When at last I roared she would have called
the younger wenche but I admired her
and bade her owne two hands supplye.

The waitinge girle stood holding linens
while my tranquille nurse displayed
and crowed when it was done.

Oh warme releef, sappe
bloominge up my stalke again.
And so the tulippe cured me.

## Marzipan

You stood
unwrapping
marzipan.
The skin
of wedding
cakes.
Almonds
and sugar
disappointed
you.
Salt.
Do
you
still
want
my
plain
body?
Once
you
told me
no.
Now,
let my
lips
reach across,
commit
what
we
both knew
never was
impossible

## Yoga Camp

Workmen had been in;
lifting the toilet seat
playing with the gongs
napping on the zafus  –   now
three yoginis are burning
sage and sandalwood
chattering
against the hard debris
of boots, cans of pop, cheap newspapers.
They ask themselves,
how did these men get here?
why choose our caravan?
When the last transparent cake
wrapper
has been shoved in the bin
the youngest      (when
she hears it starting up)
walks over to the van
one hand      lifting
her saffron robe      from her toes
to her ankles      for speed –
(it's hot and she's carrying
a bottle of sparkling water)
that man –
the young one
sitting in the back   –
the one who drank from her neti bowl,
he bothers her.

## The Case for Eventual Orgasm

Favourite position:
mountain pose – erect,
adapted *paryankasana*
"bed, couch or sofa pose"
your face
turning black,
concentrating over me
like the Aeon Girl.
One stroke
every thousand years
until the mountain
wears away.
Scree
trembles;
mountains
move
when
the Aeon Girl
walks near;
taking off her shawl
patient,
light,
steady,
stroking orchids
with her hips –
rock
with her scarf
every
thousand years.

## Yahaba - Where We Met

That afternoon
        we slept *before*
making love, when I woke
your breasts were as warm as a beach;
        lightly
the clouds moved over you,
   lightly their shadows
changed,  matching
   the shallow tide.   The bed's odd
independence – how the sheets
        settle at your hip,
           headboard
and pillows alive –
           your thirst
and mine
        not knowing where we squeeze
              for moisture.
   I remember Yahaba
   where we met – passing
   blankets through the window –
   the moon above the rice fields
   where we slept.
        Cedar buckets
        cedar baths – leaking in torrents
until the red wood expands and we bathe
        together
– gardens on one side,
   – cool, enormous rooms
              on the other.

## After Forty Years

Time melts,
   you
   never were
ratcheted away.
   I remember everything –
     tongue and lips
  and now your thighs
   trembling
      at seventy.     Returning
      we both    agree
   to re-enlist
as agents
   of the body's mad demands.
When I first saw you,
   struck in the solar plexus
by an opening door,      it
      never closed.
   We both obeyed
   some backbone then.
   Again
    we spend our money
on drinks we don't recognise;
     going on unfamiliar tears
  to kiss a pool of water;
   drink deep
    at the blue
    god's
      fountain.

Keith Bayliss was born in Swansea in 1954, studied in Swansea and Sheffield and has been a professional artist since 1977. He has a wide experience of working through the arts with the community and education, both as an artist and independent projects organiser. He has written extensively on artists and the arts in education. He exhibits widely and has spent many years working with artists and writers from Wales and Europe, developing collaborative links that have created opportunities for exhibitions and publications.

The work for *Weak Eros* is a direct response to the words of David Greenslade.